TECHNIC

**David Carr Glover
and Jay Stewart**

Design and Illustrations: Jeannette Aquino
Editor: Carole Flatau

FOREWORD

Teacher and Parents:

This TECHNIC book provides interesting musical studies to develop the student's technical facility at the keyboard. The material reinforces music fundamentals and concepts presented at this level of study.

The teacher should encourage the student to explore various tempos and dynamics. Students should be constantly aware of posture and hand position as they practice these studies.

This TECHNIC book is correlated page by page with the LESSONS book and other supplementary materials recommended for this level. It may also be used with other methods of piano study.

Each piece should be introduced with the method as indicated.

Supplementary materials correlated with
LESSONS, Level Two, from the
David Carr Glover METHOD for PIANO

Additional teaching aids include
Music Assignment Book, Music Flash Cards,
Manuscript Writing Book

Contents

COSMIC COWBOY

Interval of a 6th

GLOVER - STEWART

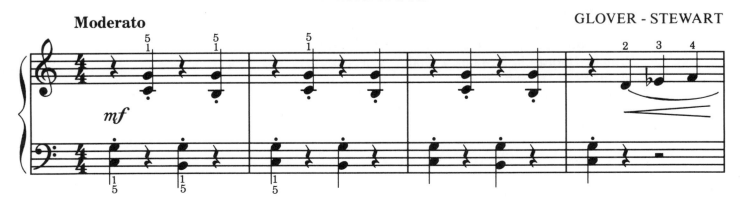

Use with page 8, LESSONS, Level Two.

6

CRAZY CLOCK

GLOVER - STEWART

Andante

Use with page 9, LESSONS, Level Two.

WOODEN SHOES

POGO STICK

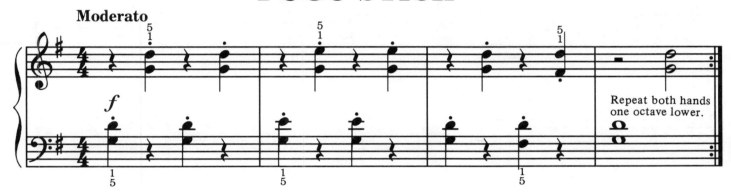

HELICOPTER

Use with page 10, LESSONS, Level Two.

THE MONSTER WALTZ

GLOVER - STEWART

Use with page 11, LESSONS, Level Two.

TONE BALANCE (Review)

Many times one hand will play louder than the other. This is called TONE BALANCE.

FREIGHT TRAIN BLUES

Interval of a 7th

GLOVER - STEWART

Moderato

Use with page 12, LESSONS, Level Two.

STRETCHING
Interval of an 8th (Octave)

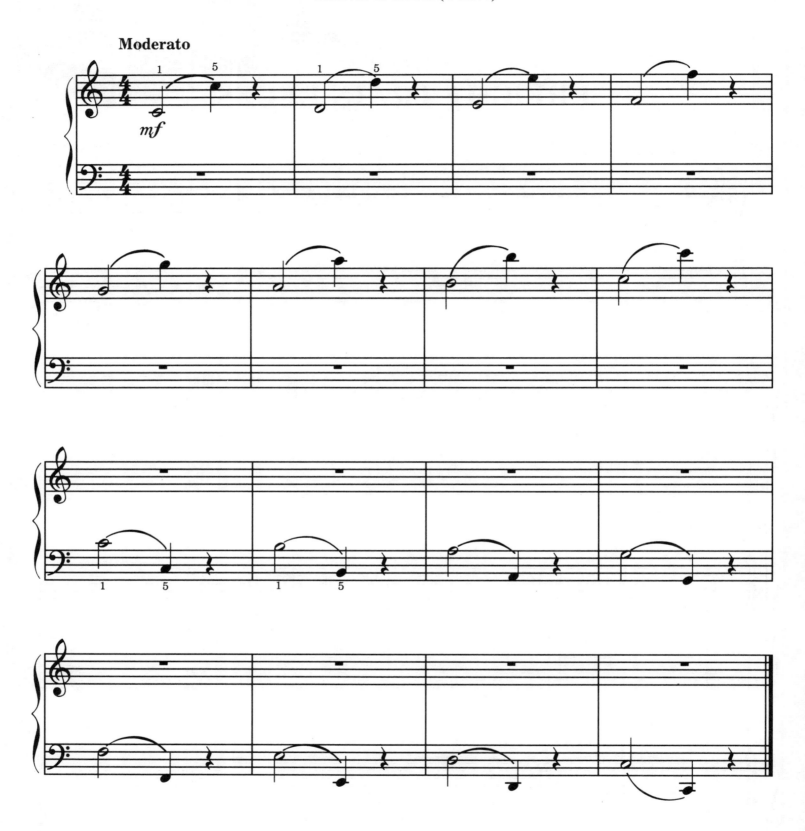

TEACHER: This octave study may be played divided between the hands if the student cannot comfortably reach an octave.

Use with page 13, LESSONS, Level Two.

TETRACHORDS

Major Scales

Stems up - R.H.
Stems down - L.H.

Use with pages 16-17, LESSONS, Level Two.

12

TRIADS

Two or more intervals played together (harmonically) form a chord.
A TRIAD is a three-note chord.

TURNING CARTWHEELS

Use with pages 18-19, LESSONS, Level Two.

PRIMARY CHORDS

Triads built on the first, fourth and fifth tones (degrees) of the scale are called PRIMARY CHORDS. They are identified by Roman numerals and by letter names.

GET READY!

GET SET!

GO!

Use with page 20, LESSONS, Level Two.

CHORD PROGRESSIONS

The change from one chord to another is called a CHORD PROGRESSION.

POPCORN

C Major Chord Progression
I - IV - I

GLOVER - STEWART

Use with page 22, LESSONS, Level Two.

JUMPING JACKS

C Major Chord Progression
I - V - I

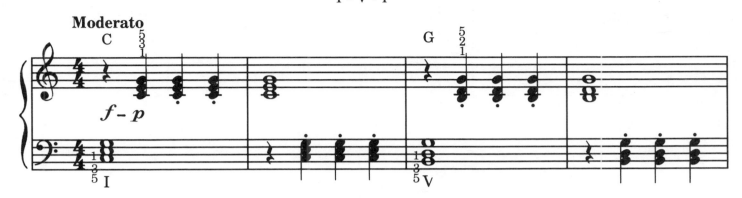

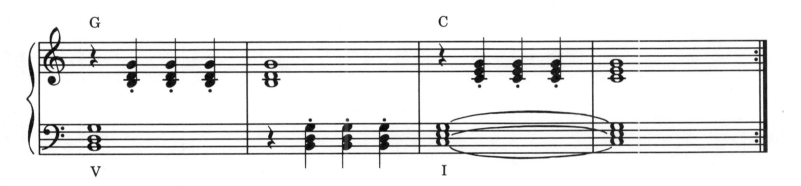

TENNIS

C Major Chord Progression
I - V - I

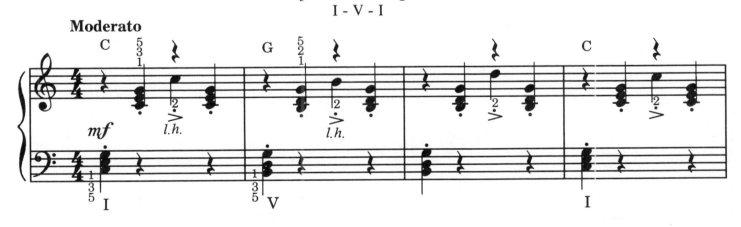

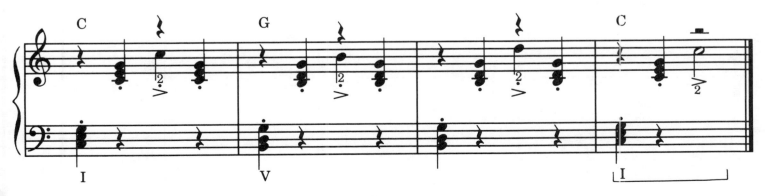

Use with page 23, LESSONS, Level Two.

C MAJOR CHORD PROGRESSION

I - IV - I - V - I

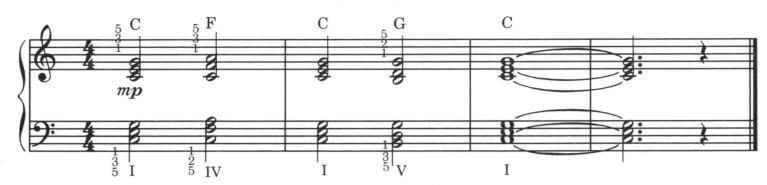

RACING

C Major Chord Progression
I - IV - I - V - I

Use with pages 24-25, LESSONS, Level Two.

C MAJOR CHORD PROGRESSION
I - V7 - I

THE TRAIN

C Major Chord Progression
I - V7 - I

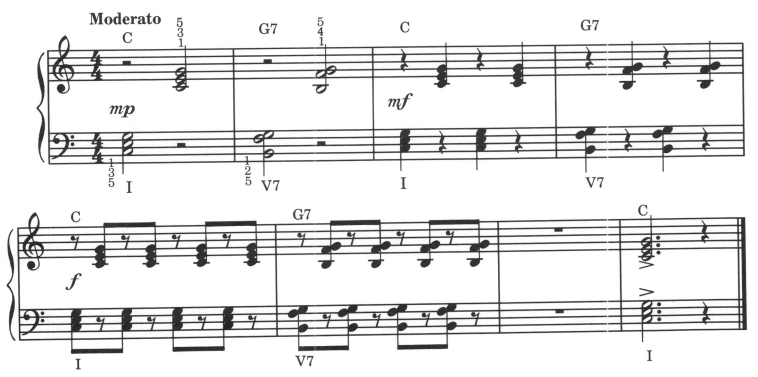

Use with pages 26-27, LESSONS, Level Two.

STRUTTIN' DOWN MAIN STREET

G Major Chord Progression

I - V7 - I

Use with page 28, LESSONS, Level Two.

THE SWISS YODELER

F Major Chord Progression
I - V7 - I

GLOVER - STEWART

Use with page 29, LESSONS, Level Two.

C MAJOR CHORD PROGRESSION
I - IV - I - V7 - I

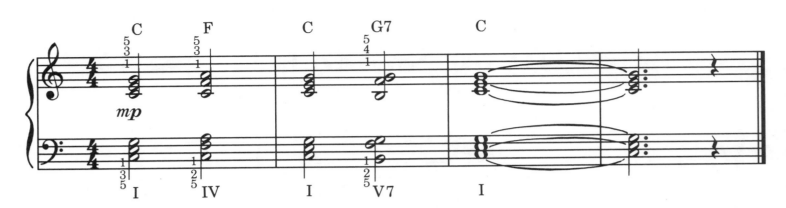

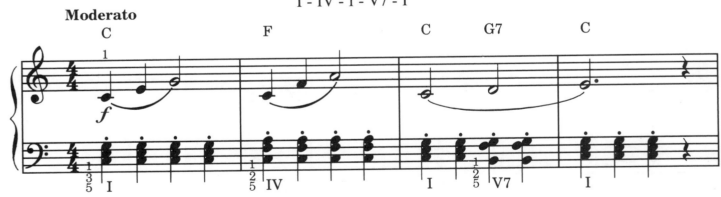

MARCH OF THE METRONOMES
C Major Chord Progression
I - IV - I - V7 - I

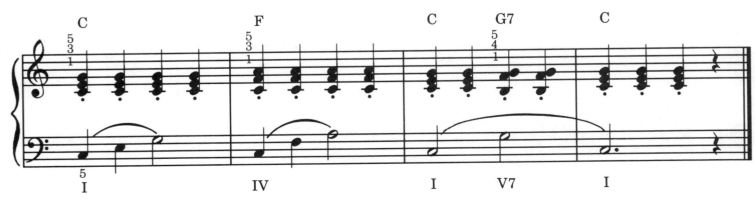

Use with page 30, LESSONS, Level Two.

G MAJOR CHORD PROGRESSION
I - IV - I - V7 - I

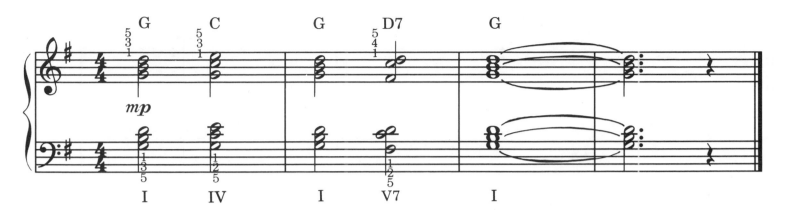

RUSH HOUR
G Major Chord Progression
I - IV - I - V7 - I

Allegro

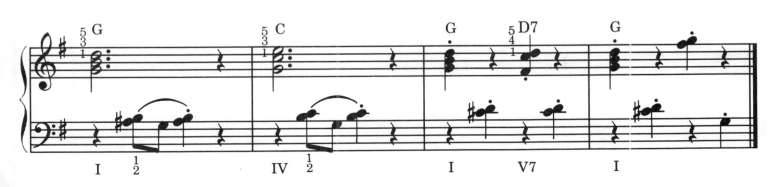

Use with page 31, LESSONS, Level Two.

F MAJOR CHORD PROGRESSION
I - IV - I - V7 - I

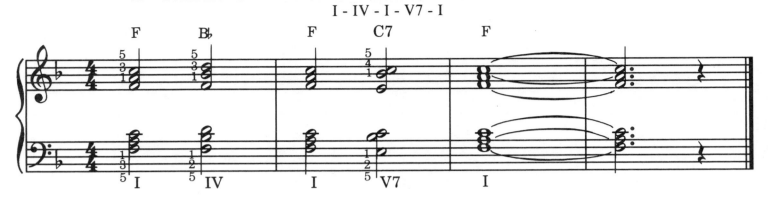

TWINKLE, TWINKLE, LITTLE ROCK STAR

F Major Chord Progression
I - IV - I - V7 - I

Allegro

Use with page 32, LESSONS, Level Two.

D MAJOR TETRACHORDS
D Major Scale

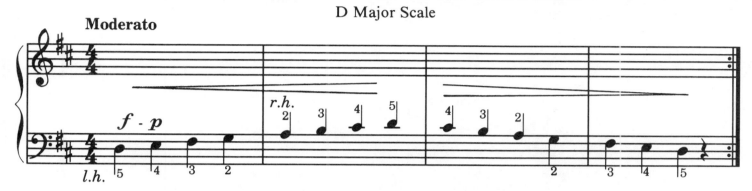

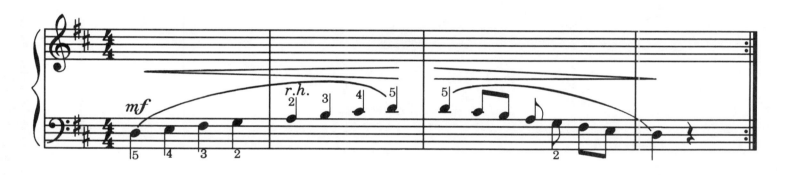

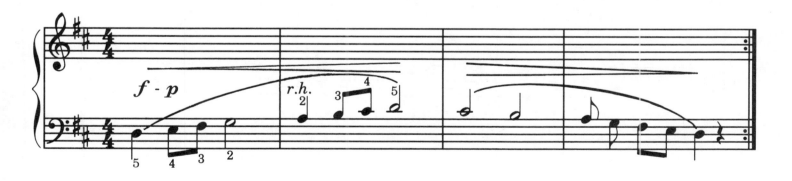

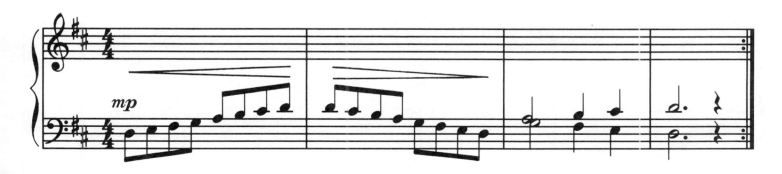

Use with pages 33-34, LESSONS, Level Two.

D MAJOR CHORD PROGRESSION
I - IV - I - V7 - I

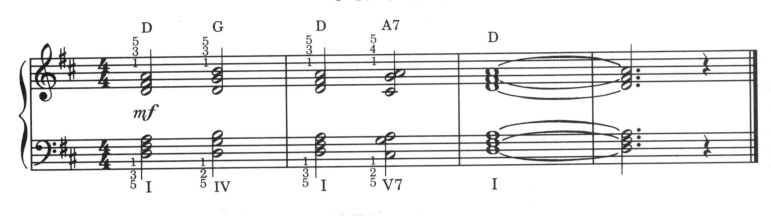

ALPINE DANCE

D Major Chord Progression
I - IV - I - V7 - I

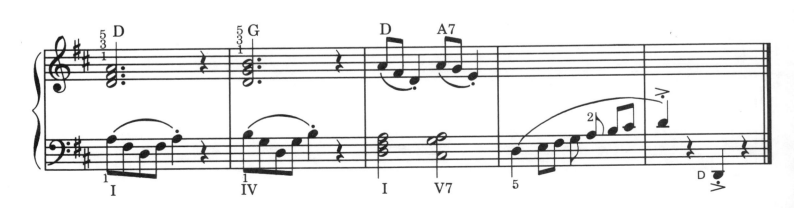

Use with page 35, LESSONS, Level Two.

PREPARATION FOR PLAYING
C - G - D MAJOR SCALES

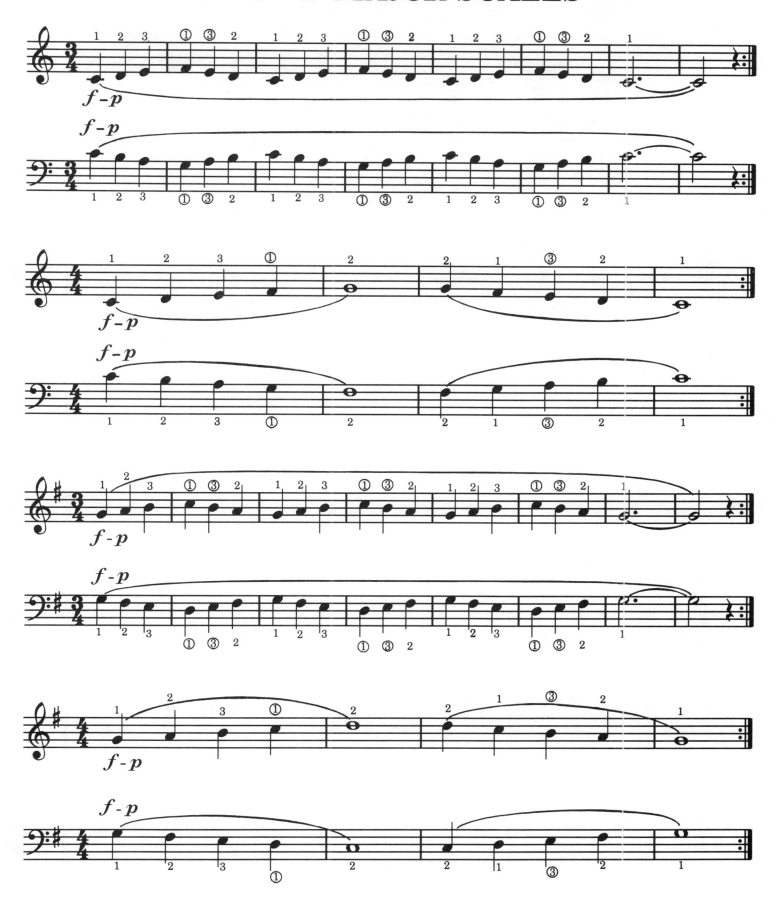

TEACHER: These exercises should be transposed to the key of D Major.

Use with pages 38-39, LESSONS, Level Two.

C MAJOR SCALE

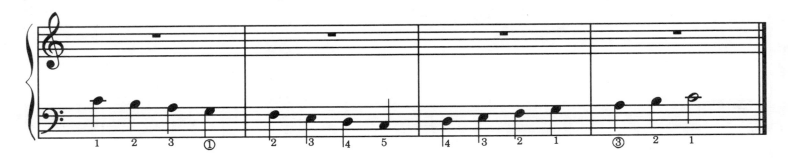

Contrary Motion

Parallel Motion

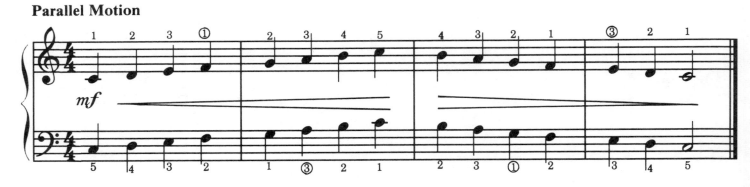

Use with pages 41-43, LESSONS, Level Two.

PRIMARY CHORDS IN C MAJOR

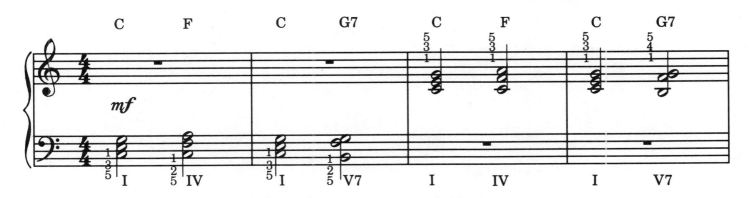

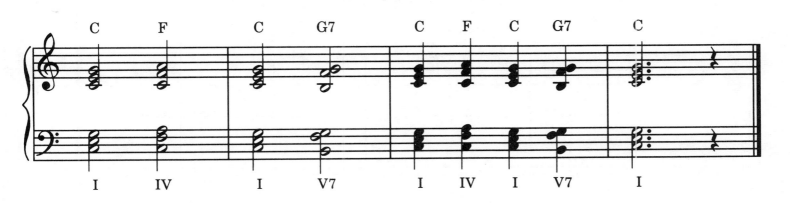

C MAJOR ARPEGGIO

Stems up - R.H.
Stems down - L.H.

Use with pages 41-43, LESSONS, Level Two.

G MAJOR SCALE

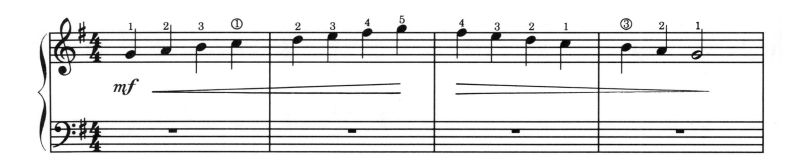

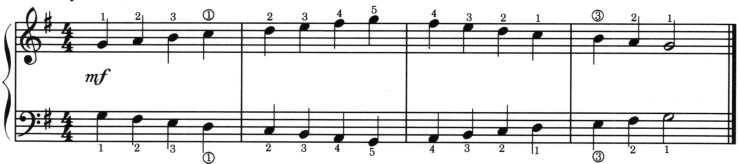

Contrary Motion

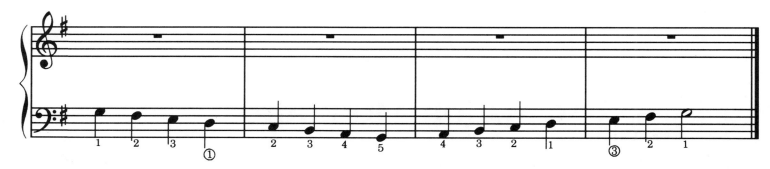

Parallel Motion

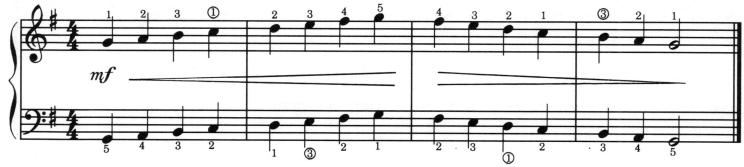

Use with pages 44-45, LESSONS, Level Two.

PRIMARY CHORDS IN G MAJOR

G MAJOR ARPEGGIO

Stems up - R.H.
Stems down - L.H.

Use with pages 44-45, LESSONS, Level Two.

D MAJOR SCALE

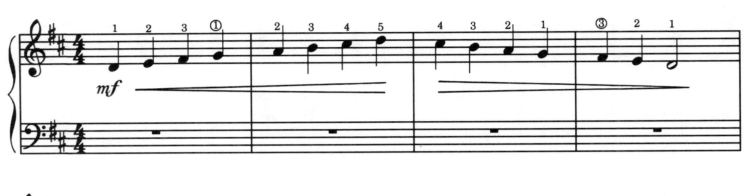

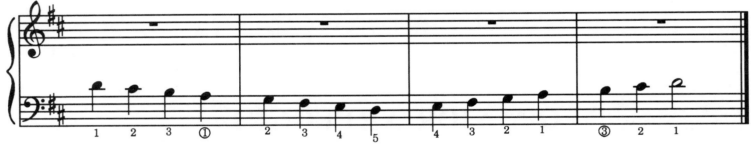

Contrary Motion

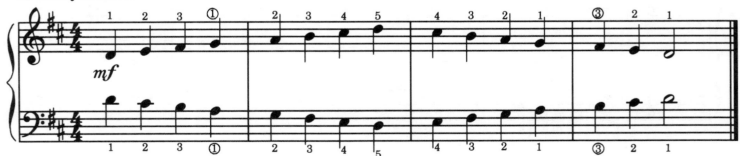

Parallel Motion

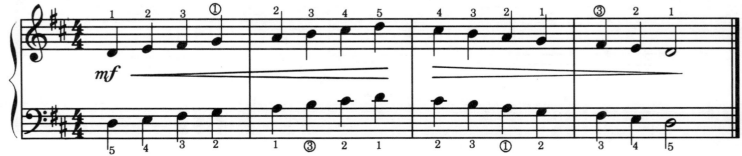

Use with pages 46-47, LESSONS, Level Two.

PRIMARY CHORDS IN D MAJOR

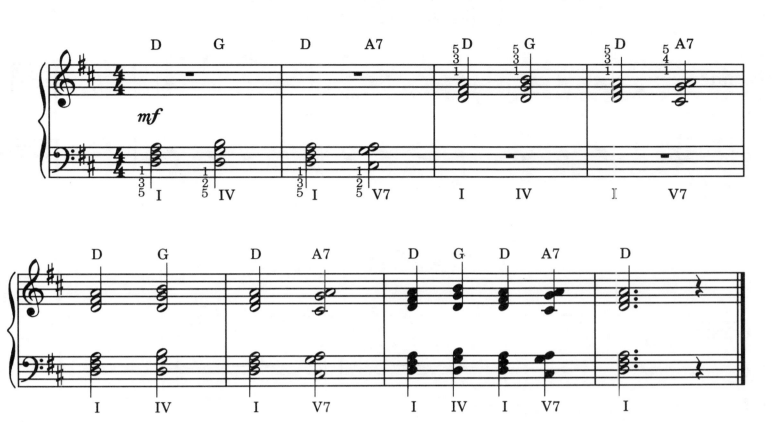

D MAJOR ARPEGGIO

Stems up - R.H.
Stems down - L.H.

Use with pages 46-47, LESSONS, Level Two.

PREPARATION FOR PLAYING
F MAJOR SCALE

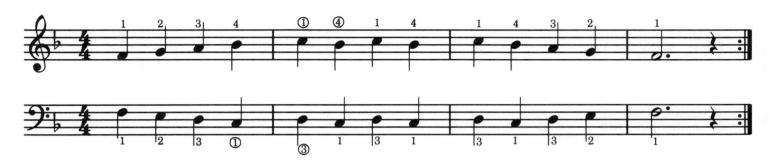

F MAJOR SCALE

Contrary Motion

Parallel Motion

Use with pages 48-49, LESSONS, Level Two.

PRIMARY CHORDS IN F MAJOR

F MAJOR ARPEGGIO

Stems up - R.H.
Stems down - L.H.

Use with pages 48-49, LESSONS, Level Two.

MINOR POSITIONS AND CHORDS

C Minor

D Minor

F Minor

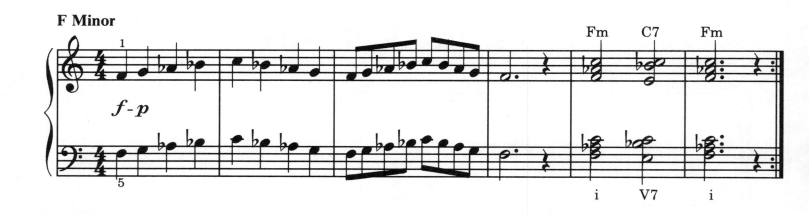

G Minor

Use with pages 50-54, LESSONS, Level Two.